Thousandfold

Nina Bogin, poet and translator, was born in New York City and has lived in France since 1976. Her previous collections are In the North, The Winter Orchards and The Lost Hare. In addition to numerous translations in the domain of art history, her translation of The Illiterate by Agota Kristof was published in 2013.

Thousandfold

Nina Bogin

CARCANET

ACKNOWLEDGEMENTS

Some of these poems first appeared in PN *Review*, *Little Star*
and *New Walk Magazine*.

With my thanks to Beverley Bie Brahic, Linda Zisquit and
Magda Bogin.

First published in Great Britain in 2019 by
Carcanet
Alliance House, 30 Cross Street
Manchester M2 7AQ
www.carcanet.co.uk

Book design by Andrew Latimer
Printed in Great Britain by SRP Ltd., Exeter, Devon

The publisher acknowledges financial
assistance from Arts Council England.

Supported using public funding by
ARTS COUNCIL
ENGLAND

MIX
Paper from
responsible sources
FSC® C014540

Contents

Thousandfold   13

Landscape   14

The Hawk   15

The Roe Stag   17

The Winter Fox   18

At the Bend   19

A Story   21

Two Horses   22

Welcome   23

Rain   24

Springtime, Germany   26

Visit to a Friend   27

Knowledge   31

Birthday   33

The Bees   35

Saintpaulia Ballerina   37

The White Month   39

Chores   43

Fractal   44

The Farrier   45

Seeds   47

The Egg   49

Night Sounds   51

Mending   52

The Sheepskin Coat   53

Pink   54

Practical Joke   55

Feathers   56

The Golden Oriole   58

Cleaning the Hibiscus   59

Sleepless   60
Kettle   61
August 6   62
Here: an Alphabet   63
Hallowe'en   66
Dementia   68
Fish   70
K.   71
The House Shrew   73
Slippers   74
Daylight Saving   76
Evenings with Mika   77
Le Quatrième Internationale   79
Everlasting   81
Spice Cupboard   82
The Manor House   84

Note   87

for MILENA and ANTONIN

and in memory of my husband
ALAIN BUTTARD

Abrikostraerne findes, abrikostraerne findes
(Apricot trees exist, apricot trees exist)
    INGER CHRISTENSEN, *Alphabet*
    translated from the Danish by Susanna Nied

One cannot live without hope. One must have hope. [...] And
my eternal theme is the struggle between good and evil. Evil
may be more prevalent in the world, but good is more concen-
trated. Nihilism and pessimism are easier because they require
no effort. I go through pessimism finally to confirm at the end
that I say 'Yes' until my last breath to the beauty of the world.
    PETERIS VASKS, composer
    conversation with John Kehoe
    Berlin, 26 November 1994

Thousandfold

Thousandfold

Thousandfold the light
encompasses us

patiently
against our mortal

impatience.
We are human,

thus destitute.
Awkward we fumble

with our small
offerings

to the everyday,
crumbs, petals, dust.

What do we sift over,
what should we keep,

what turn to gold,
give thanks for,

render thousandfold
to light?

Landscape

In ash winter
I drive between snowfields

down the grey highway.
On either side of the river

snow abolishes
tow paths and bridges,

road-signs and place-names.
In this perfectly swept world

where I keep watch
there are no fissures,

no asperities,
only the winding river,

the steep white hillsides
and, scribbled at the top,

the black ink of the evergreens.

The Hawk

1

This is her chosen tree,
the ash. This meadow, copse
and stream, her fief.
A dowdy queen,
she commands
from ground and branch.
Everything she needs is here –
mice for hunger,
water for thirst.
I admire
her single-minded purpose,
how she glides along the slope
when it thaws, or settles
her weighty robe of feathers
on a patch of grass,
snapping her head
to the quiver of a mouse.
She is never
at a loss.
Time thief,
every minute is hers.
No waste, no distractions.
I could do as well
to fill
all the moments of the day –
my life –
with her acuity!

2

Her wingspan's as big
as a house.
When she swerves down
for the catch,
her burnished-brown
wings outstretched,
I'm unnerved – or is it she?
Safe indoors,
I'm small as a mouse.
She fixes her eye on me.
We keep our distance,
our see-saw harmony

of sliding proportions.
We will never be friends.
Neighbors, rather,
with a tree in common.
My stately ash
is her observatory.
She sits on a low branch,
grey and solitary.
I watch her from the kitchen.
Caution is our credo.
These are the limits of empathy.

The Roe Stag

Between birches, the roe stag
steps across hard snow.
His lichen, bark and moss
are sealed in ice.
This is winter's law.

He's alone this season;
it has been planned thus.
His antlers – stag's
mask – will defend his doe
and fawns' terrain

in spring.
That is his task.
Today he will not eat.
He dreams
of musk-scent, sap-flow.

He stamps on ice,
waits for thaw.
He knows where to go,
what to do.
If only I also knew.

The Winter Fox

A morning in December, fog-lost.
The roads are hushed

with hoar-frost. Cautiously
we climb, one car after another,

to the crest between two valleys,
two silver-clouded meadows.

It's here, where it was struck,
that a fox lies across the road,

its still-lithe body –
limbs, paws, muzzle, belly –

sprawled intact. Oh
foolish beast,

how ill you timed
your morning jaunt!

Your fur glistens
with dawn's snow,

in first light.
The cars drive past.

At the Bend

The sisters at the bend,
when their aged mother died
(she used to sit beneath
the eaves, staring
out across the road),
sold off all the land
to developers :
three semi-detached,
four individual houses
at affordable rents
plumb in the middle
of a meadow
prone to floods.

          Semis
lugging truckload after
truckload of cinder-blocks,
roofing, concrete, have
gouged out the roadside
at the bend and, by the by,
razed the centenary
hornbeam hedge,
home to blackbirds,
blue-tits, wrens,
flattening the remains
of splintered roots and stumps
into mud, where
deep-sunk tire-tracks now
fill up with snow.

                    The sisters
aren't fazed. To hell
with the meadow,
the hedges and the birds.
Property is money,
as everybody knows.
In the back garden,
a row of fresh facades
and picture windows
meets their gaze.
In front, come summer,
they'll hang out their sheets,
pot blood-red geraniums,
sit as always under the eaves
and watch the new neighbors'
cars round the bend
like so many
well-earned dividends.

A Story

August night. The sky unwinds
its skeins of light.

The tiniest of stars
slip through our fingers,

galaxies rest on our palms.
Layer on layer of blackness,

drifts of white
to plunge our hands in,

shake out like feathers,
 flurries of stars

familiar and untamed.
It's a story being told,

forever
and at this very moment.

No matter that I can't understand.
Wordless, I begin

all over again,
in a newfound language

where everything
is waiting to be named.

Two Horses

Two horses graze in a high meadow,
their necks bent to winter grass.

Blessed are they among the animals,
so much closer to the light.

Welcome

for Milena

Welcome, child.
Bienvenue!
Welcome to all things
as small as you,

poppy seeds, ladybugs,
drops of rain.
More than a thought,
less than a name,

your task is simple :
to become.
But take your time!
You've only just begun.

Welcome to all
that is slow,
snails and stars
and falling snow,

sky and wind,
tree and bird,
and for each one
a chosen word.

The world is as old
as you are new.
Welcome, little one,
bienvenue.

Rain

Not yet
forty days and forty nights,

not a deluge nor even a brimming river,
but rain, ever-present as light

and taking the place of light,
thick rolls of clouds, blue-grey,

advancing from the west
like the Atlantic Ocean

come inland to engulf us
with flood tides, spring winds.

Thus is a tempest unleashed.
Leaves, grass, flowers

overflow, weigh down branches,
grow knee-deep overnight;

buttercups float
on estuaries of green.

Will we drown
in lilac, apple-blossoms,

forget-me-nots, as the Gulf Stream
veers from its course?

Today on my morning run,
between rain-showers,

I watched mottled clouds
stream over the hills,

saw pink apple-petals,
wind-strewn,

lined up one by one
in eddies along the brook,

peered down from the bridge
and saw two ducks

among the rushes,
one behind the other,

their sleek heads bobbing metal-green.
They paddled, idled.

Two ducks.
Two by two.

And you,
my friend, without whom –

we too shall board the ark.

Springtime, Germany

We pass through the patient countryside.
Horses stand in fields, their ears twitching.
Cars idle at train-crossings.

Everything could go wrong, but nothing is amiss.
A man on a path watches the train go by,
shielding his eyes with his hand.

The bright-colored factories and parked cars
are all in place, carefully aligned.
These are rules that we obey.

But the leaves, the dark-veined leaves
crowding into the morning sky –
the leaves spread anarchy.

Visit to a Friend

for Claire Fagnart

I   *The Dream*

I take a snow shovel, a laundry rack and my older daughter,
and on foot we struggle along the beach to reach the town.
There's no snow, but the sand makes walking difficult
and it takes a long time to cross the cove,
longer than we expected, as often happens in dreams.
When we get to your building, it's suppertime.
I leave the shovel and rack in the entrance, by the stairwell –
why did I bring them anyway?
They won't be of any use to you –
and we climb the creaking stairs. It's important
to announce our presence with two loud knocks
on the wooden door, but instead there's a heavy drape
and knocking just makes it sway.
We can hear voices from inside – the children
gathered around the supper table.
Calling out 'Hello!' we push aside the curtain
and your young daughter runs to greet us. And you?
You're busy at the sink, and now that I'm awake
I'm not sure whether you were glad we came, or not.

II   *The Cove*

I recognize the cove. It's Quettehou
on the Normandy coast, where years ago
our two families spent a week
in your aunt's cottage. The light over the bay
was golden, muted. At low tide
we wandered for miles on the sand
past beached boats, oyster beds.
Inland, the meadows were drenched green.
We ate fresh fish, rich cream. Our lives
seemed bountiful, blessed – and they were.

III   *The Arrival*

It came at a snail's pace, sickly-silver,
incremental; like all disasters,
it caught you unawares.
There were signs, naturally, but
you read them only later.
A gratuitous irony –
the boy you thought was saved,
who stood, we deemed,
on high ground –
it was he who floundered.

IV   *Happiness*

The hourglass of happiness is shattered.
Its fine grains grate beneath our soles.
Happiness? It's what we acknowledge
once it's fled. Peals of laughter.
Shrugs of shoulders. Little dramas
we were able to tame. Whatever it was,
we didn't know – how could we? –
what we'd be up against, or whether
we'd be equal to the task.
And there would be
no choice. It would be given,
to leave or to take –
a comfortless,
timeless wisdom.

V   *Filles du Calvaire*

In an earlier life, in Paris
in our *chambres de bonne*,
we were inseparable.
People took us for sisters –
our long brown hair, long skirts,
our reckless naiveté.
I admired how you called
a spade a spade,
your *franc parler*.
I was older, but you
were more daring, more sure.
Do you remember we three
sitting on the métro, you, me,
and a *dramaturg* from East Berlin

who was courting us both
for one drawn-out evening,
going from your place to mine
and finally to Saint-Germain-des-Prés
where we eventually took leave of him
or he of us? The stations flashed past –
Bastille, Chemin Vert, Filles du Calvaire.
And you said – it had been
an unforgiving year –
'Je suis une fille du Calvaire.'
I am a daughter of Calvary.
You did not explain.
Our suitor was intrigued, which may
or may not have been your aim.
As for me, I was impressed
by your sense of drama,
your nerve –
something akin to
comedy, though dark.
It was as if, even then –
I see this now – you knew
that the price of experience
was pain, and chose
to laugh at it.
I avoided – do I still? –
such stark realities.
It's this, perhaps, that's made us
what we are, for better or for worse,
along with – as you often say –
chance, which plays a silent role
that neither I nor you
can ascertain or even wish to.

Knowledge

For Kate Cowser, 1941 – 2013

How much she knew!
Knew from the beginning
what we would not admit.
We hoped; she knew.
The knowledge of it
changed her from within.
A calm and fragile beauty
came to sculpt her face,
deepened her eyes, gave her
a gentle, tremulous smile.
She was like a candle, burning.

Death was not kind to her,
it didn't care. But she
was kind to it. She made
no fuss, no demands.
Her thoughts were for
her husband, her family,
her friends. Look after him,
she said. She bade
each one farewell.
These were the gifts
she bestowed at parting.

Now her ashes rest,
as they should,
in her dearest places.
I water her plants and flowers,
keep an eye on the house.
I hear her voice in lively

conversation, her greeting
at my door.
Hers was a life
well-lived, hard-earned.
What she taught us, only
now are we learning.

Birthday

for Antonin

First of all, on a January morning,
there will be a jigsaw-puzzle of clouds
in winter colors of pink and gold,
violet and blue – puzzle-pieces
that will drift apart as the sky
lightens into day.
Then, where the road winds down
into the city, a jagged line
of Alps will rise up
on the farthest edge of the horizon
and disappear just as suddenly
after the descent into the valley,
where crows in whirlwinds of black
will loop over the houses,
and a solitary heron,
slow and heavy in its horizontal sweep,
will lift its wings
and head west along the canal,
away from the city. There will be
cars and trucks, tumbledown farmhouses
and new apartment flats, bushes and hedges,
apple trees and clotheslines,
a black dog barking at the end of a chain,
bus stops and bicyclers, passengers and passersby,
bakeries and flower shops, hair salons,
repair shops, supermarkets, parking lots,
shopping carts filled to the brim
on a single January morning
in the ebb and flow of an overcrowded world
where, all the same, there will be room

for you with your wide-open gaze
and a lifetime ahead of you
all your own.

The Bees

Startled
by a distant humming

on a windy morning
in June,

I saw moving towards me
in the unsettled air

a tornado
of bees

bristling
with electricity,

a hundred
or a thousand bees

sweeping across
the parking lot

towards the alders
by the river.

They passed me by,
a wild chorus

battling and buzzing,
then rose in unison

to the top of a tree
and circled there.

I walked on
in the warm wind

that wrapped itself
around me

as if I too
were part of the air

and would arrive
and disappear

with no more claim
on the passage of time

than a dust-mote
or a drifting seed,

and I could still
hear the bees –

the otherworldly chant
of their plainsong,

the metal clamor
of their wings.

Saintpaulia Ballerina

Because we can't
write this poem
together, you and I,
who didn't like
each other,
I must write it
for you – who
will never read it.
I have, you know,
your flower.
It brings
an obligation
you couldn't have
foreseen.
I took it as
a peace offering
after that stormy
end-of-semester.
You handed it to me
on the stairs,
with a muffled
explanation.
A truce of sorts.
A gift. A gesture.
An ordinary African
violet, with felt-like
dull-green leaves
and dainty, ballerina-pink
flowers that twirled
and unfurled
in the slanted light

of the window.
They blossom now
with startling
regularity.
To be honest,
I didn't like
to have a flower
that made me
think of you.
But I liked the pink,
frail, determined
ballerina-flowers.
And a flower's needs
must be obeyed.
I don't shrink
from yours.
I water it each day
by the kitchen window
and yes, I think
of you, more often
than I'd like,
and the enigma
of your life,
how in oblivion
you lived
your last days
in a hospital
bed, tended by
your husband,
your infant child.
The water streams
from the spout
of the green
watering can.

The White Month

Winter

Quarter moons and half-moons,
waxing and waning through bitter skies.
Snowfall. Thaw. Frost. Rain.
Arrows of sunlight through charcoal clouds.
Sundown's fuchsia flames.
Twilight. Night. Hidden stars.
Silent dawns. Gentle rustlings of birds.

Window

Squirreled indoors, peeling off
the paper-thin leaves of Brussels sprouts
with the old paring knife. Scent of green.
Faint sunlight at the kitchen window.
Flurry of feathers as blue tits and finches
skid across the stone table strewn with seeds.

Song

An east wind. Mustard-yellow sunlight
zigzags across trees and hills.
The air is fresh as running water.
High in the branches, magpies chatter.
Blackbirds in the hornbeam hedge
send out their liquid, hopeful song.
Long is the month of January.
Boundless the patience of the birds.

Crows

Afternoon hushed and shuttered.
Snow-light. Crows caw from one
tree-top to another. They're always
at the ready, flying off in twos
or threes, dropping down
on different branches to converse
and complain. With all their fuss
and natter, who takes any
notice of them now, like the boy
who cried wolf, the girl
who claimed the house was on fire?

Frugal

Frugal are the days
of January
doling out
their sober light
on flattened grass,
dull-brown hills.
We lie low,
assailed
by dark visions.
But now the snow
glides in
with a light
of its own,
swan-white,
effortless,
falling
as if it had all

the time in the world,
and stillness
to heal
the most fretful
of souls.

Houses

Crystal-sharp air over
fallen snow. Spice-scent
of wood smoke. We walk
along the brook. Snowflakes
drift down from the north,
from the west. The everyday
houses are softened, as if
at last they could bring comfort
to the people who live there.

Tracks

Trees sink down under snow.
The day draws out
into paler blue, wisps of grey.
Tracks crisscross the meadow,
intersect, run parallel -
deer, fox, mouse, squirrel,
birds of every feather,
cats from all the houses.
And who can say
those staggered imprints
emerging from the hedge
are not the tracks

of the hare we'll never see
who, alert to every danger,
quivering with fear,
musters its courage
and boldly leaps
across the snow at night
when we are fast asleep?

Thaw

Sunlight warms us at midday.
Through the melting snow,
patches of grass spread out
like the maps of a new country,
with rivers and meadows,
lowlands and wetlands,
estuaries opening out to the sea…
 But the world is old.
It waits for us
as it has always waited.
And we are too late.

Chores

Lavender-scented laundry
to hang up to dry.
Airing of bedclothes
by the open window.
Plumping of pillows,
straightening of sheets.
Vacuuming in and out
of the rooms,
stirring up a storm.
Whisk of the broom
through the kitchen,
in the corners,
behind the doors.
Mopping of the floors.
Dust-shake.
Sponge-swipe.
Carrots to scrub.
Onions to slice.
Water to bring to a boil.
Tasks, chores,
the ordinary toil
that takes us
by the scruff of the neck,
squares our shoulders,
sets us straight.
How else
would the job get done?

Fractal

I take a head of Romanesco cauliflower,
weigh it in my hand,
admire the enchanted forest
on its own island.
Each pale-green floweret
contains a smaller version
of itself, over and over,
down to the tiniest replica
my eyes can barely see.
I think of Mandelbrot,
Fibonacci, golden
numbers, imperfect
symmetries.
It gives one pause,
standing at the kitchen counter,
to think of infinity,
knowing that the world,
obeying different sets of rules,
isn't subject to purely
human destiny.
But here at the cutting board
where science and philosophy
meet, I can go no further.
I lift the chef's knife,
chop the fractals
into edible portions
and tip them
into the steamer.

The Farrier

Because I had announced
with wild confidence
and joyful generosity –
almost with glee –
that I would shoe anyone's horse
that needed shoeing – I'd done,
it seemed, a training course –
the girls began to arrive
with their geldings, their mares,
leading them on long ropes,
and suddenly I realized
that I didn't remember
how to shoe horses, didn't even have
the material – I began to search
on the shelves for the nails,
the pincers, the rasp, and where
were the horse-shoes,
and the hammer and the anvil
that probably I couldn't wield, let alone
hold the horse's hoof on my knee,
oh, and the forge, and the tongs,
what about that? –
but the girls kept arriving
with their sleek horses –
a shining roan, a glossy black –
and when I tried to explain
that it would be a terrible mistake
for me to shoe their horses, given
that I didn't have the first idea
of how to go about it, they said
I couldn't do that to them,

their horses needed to be shod
because they had a jumping event
that very afternoon, and I had promised.
I knew I'd lose the respect
of all my friends, old and new,
saw how irresponsible I'd been,
how boastful and incompetent –
how was it possible I hadn't
foreseen the consequences,
even in a dream?

Seeds

1

The seeds
moved in a crowd.

They pushed
and shoved,

elbowed,
jostled.

Each wanted
a place in the sun.

2

Let us be seeds.
Seed one, seed two.

Yellow
and smooth.

Pointed
at both ends.

Glossy,
slippery,

very
small.

Let us
think

ourselves
into seeds.

Without husk
or chaff,

pod
or shell.

Simply
to be

little seed you,
little seed me.

Hard
and sleek,

with no special
needs.

Is it not good
to be a seed?

The Egg

for Milena

You finger
the bird's egg found
last summer.
Half an egg,
to be precise.
Milk-white, frayed
at the edges, it sits
just inside the flowerpot
of the rosary vine.
Pale-green string
of hearts, pure white
eggshell nestled
on potting soil.
You say you don't
have an egg at home.
How touching
you don't ask for it
outright.
I think you know
what eggs are like.
At home the egg
will crack or break
and you'll be sad.
I say we'll look
for another egg
in springtime
and it'll be
your own bird's egg,
your first,

pale-blue or cream
or speckled-white.
Today, a half year
gone, we found
near the neighbor's
pond half an eggshell,
greenish-brown.
A starling's egg,
a fledgling born,
a flight, a song —
here, Milena,
is your egg.

Night Sounds

In the renovated farmhouse we rented in those years –
all wooden paneling and rustic beams –
down in the kitchen with only the floorboards
between us, we could hear our daughters
breathing in their room upstairs,
we heard dormice scrabbling inside the walls,
hazelnuts rolling the length of the attic floor.
In winter we heard owls hooting from the woods
when the sharp black sky seemed to crackle with stars.
It was our long-lost childhood, our city-dwellers' dream…

When my parents visited from New York, we'd hear
my father pad downstairs in the middle of the night,
cautiously open the cupboard door, unscrew
the lid of a jar and screw it tightly back on.
Then, as he tiptoed up to bed,
we'd hear a sound we'll never hear again,
a sound like none other –
the crunching of a lump of brown sugar.

Mending

I'm darning tights, my daughter's
and mine, just as my mother
used to do. I use her Red Heart
black mending yarn, 20 yards,
10 cents, from what decade
I can't guess. I've inherited a bagful
of all her cards of mending wool,
Coats & Clark, Cynthia Mills,
and bits of yarn for her treasured
cashmere twin-sets, bright twists
of scarlet, canary, emerald green,
twenty, thirty years old or more.

Sweaters long worn, long gone,
tight-knit yarns to keep
the breast-bone warm, the beating heart,
the steadfast soul. I can't bear to part
with the last of her pastel sweaters
I'll never wear, pollen yellow, powder blue,
lying folded on my wardrobe shelf
in the plastic bags she carefully
wrapped them in, soft to the touch
reminders of her —
her love and ever-kindness,
my better self.

The Sheepskin Coat

Too big for me, too small for my husband,
my father's spring lamb sheepskin coat
has been hanging in our closet for over
fifteen years. It's nearly thirty years
since he died; my mother wore the coat
eleven winters more. It doesn't age,
doesn't gather dust. It's a dream
of a coat, buff-colored, warmly lined.
I take it out, try it on, look at myself
in the mirror. It sits on me like a house.
Too heavy, too wide, though my father
was short, his clothes tailored to size.
Clothes were his pride. I see him
in the sheepskin coat, his arms hanging
at his side. His thick winter gloves.
His plaid scarf. His Kangol cap.
Dressed, as always, fit to kill, elegant,
casual, as ready as he'd ever be
to face a New York winter,
the cold bite of time… If only clothes
could save a man! On the brink
of old age, illness took him in hand,
sheared the coming years off his life.
My father's coat will never fit.
It hangs on its wooden hanger
with its folds and creases,
its bulk formed to his shape,
still holding, all these years later,
his hope against hope
and all he'd have to weather.

Pink

It was her favorite color.
In the small, overheated bathroom,
pink bath rug, pink towels, pink
shower curtain, pink toilet paper…
Even now I can feel the warmth
hissing through the coils of the radiator
as I washed my hands surrounded
by pink and felt as if I might choke
if I stayed one more minute
in that narrow space –
Grandma Sophie's tiny haven
of comfort, her pastel dream
of a life without torment.
She asked for so little, only
for everyone to be happy,
or short of that,
then simply to be allowed
to wish that everyone
should be happy.
On that last visit to the apartment –
she was already ill, shrunken
in her pink bathrobe –
she followed us, my father
and me, out into the hallway
that smelled, year in, year out,
of homemade chicken soup,
and hugged me tight
whispering fiercely
into my chest
I love you I love you I love you I love you

Practical Joke

Hard to imagine
my father's father
whom I never knew
going into a corner shop
in 1934 or 1935
and saying 'I'll take
two of those' –
celluloid turds
he'd place on
the back seat of the car
before the ladies –
dressed for an outing,
his sister-in-law and wife –
got in. Oh
their shrieks!
Rubber spiders,
crouching mice –
bellyfuls of laughs!
He looks out
from a photo in sepia.
Under a perky fedora,
his apologetic, schoolboy grin.

Feathers

Who can say whether my great-great grandmothers
in Galicia or Ukraine plucked goose feathers
from snow-white geese held firmly on their knees?
No one will tell me, but I can see them
sitting on their stools with their wide laps
and heavy skirts and aprons, their fingers
plucking goose down and feathers
for pillows and coverlets and eiderdowns,
their faces worn as old linen.
In voices I can almost hear
they gossip and exclaim
about the nephew who left for America,
the daughter-in-law who's barren,
the husband who's pious
and the one who drinks too much,
their words drifting across the courtyard
into the autumn skies and clouds

as smoke curls from the chimney-tops
and mingles with the odors
of stored apples and potatoes,
fresh-cut wood and fallen leaves.
Those grandmothers with their nodding heads
and captive geese and baskets of feathers
cannot for the life of them imagine
that one day I will be sitting at a laptop
straining to hear their voices on a winter's night
in a house banked with snow
and a fire burning down to embers.

Fixed in my time as they were in theirs,
I will try to imagine my great-great grandchildren
as distant from me as tonight's scattering of stars,
and I'll wonder
who among them will think of us,
who will remember?

The Golden Oriole

There it is again, just outside
our bedroom window, at dawn –
the oriole's liquid, obsessive,
four-note song.
He's back from Africa
where he winters, in time
for an early spring.
I lift the curtain, he's flown.
Of his celebrated plumage,
its yellow, its gold,
for whole summers long
I've caught only a glimpse.
Shyness is his virtue;
he flits from tree to tree,
keeping an eye on his spouse,
his young.
But his song!
His song is an enticement,
a longing, a wish.
This is the oriole's sleight of hand,
his special trick –
to be just out of sight,
like a streak of good luck.

Cleaning the Hibiscus

It's spring-cleaning for the hibiscus –
moss is sprouting
on the old-growth branches.
This bright April morning
I put on my gardening gloves
and rub off the soft green moss.
It falls in little clumps
onto the grass. Birds sing,
blue tits whirl by, busy
with their nests, blackbirds
fluster in the bushes.
Yes, there's something
wrong with the hibiscus,
but I'm doing my best
to right it, scraping the moss,
letting the bark breathe
as I'm sure it must.
The bush is tarnished grey,
last year's pods stiff
in the air. I snap them off.
New life here, any day now!
Leaves, buds, flowers –
white with purple throats, violet-blue,
mauve, candy-striped –
they will bloom no matter what.
But the matter is not
the hibiscus, no, there is also
something amiss
with you, and about that
there is nothing
I can do.

Sleepless

4 a.m. Sounds come in single file :
one ring of the telephone,
one tap on the roof,
one bark of a deer in the woods.
How I wish it would bark again!
And that I could dream
its animal sleep
on a bed of leaves
along the stream...
Happiness has fled.
Why does it make such a difference?
Come on, take yourself in hand
and make a shopping list instead :
string to tie up the tomato plants,
a paring knife, matches, a pen,
candles and storm lamps
for the times ahead.

Kettle

Shiny black kettle, ready to whistle,
what's your tune today? You hum
over the blue flame, your breath
clouding the window-pane.
Oh kettle, you break my heart
with your lackadaisical
breakfast song, your irrepressible
bubbling-up, your steam hissing
straight into the teacup.
You'll give me the world
on a tray, happiness
in a silver spoon, bowlfuls
of wisdom and patience,
all the remedies I can sip –
such promises as you cannot keep.

August 6

On flowing
silk kimonos

graceful patterns
of plum blossoms

burned
into the skin

of the women
of Hiroshima.

Seventy years ago
today

I cannot remember
Hiroshima

but neither
can I forget.

Here: an Alphabet

Here is an ant.

Here is a bee.

Here is a beetle.

Here is a blade of grass.

Here is a burning candle.

Here is a clod of earth.

Here is a clover flower.

Here is a dandelion.

Here is an egg.

Here is a family
crossing a border.

Here is a guard
turning them back.

Here is honey
in a honeycomb.

Here is ice
on a puddle.

Here is juniper
behind a fence.

Here is a kettle
of boiling water.

Here is a lull
in a storm.

Here is a mound
where bones are buried.

Here is a nettle
to put in a soup.

Here is an opening
in a fence.

Here is a prisoner
in a camp.

Here is a quiet
nothing can disturb.

Here is a river
too wide to swim across.

Here is a stone
placed on a grave.

Here is a train
resting on a siding.

Here is an umbrella,
open, closed.

Here is a vine
growing over a wall.

Here is a wasteland
at the edge of a city.

Here is an x
to x out words.

Here is a year
and the days ahead.

Here is a zero,
the beginning

and the end.

Hallowe'en

Little girl lavender, little boy blue,
here's a pumpkin split in two,

on each side half a grin
with some teeth out and some teeth in,

a triangle nose and two wide eyes
that wink at you, that wink at you.

Here are two candles for you to light,
one for each half of a Hallowe'en night

when long-toothed shadows
flicker high and burn down low

in pumpkins that keep watch until
morning comes to windowsills.

We can't stick the two halves back
together, can't fix the marriage pact

when it goes against the grain.
What once was, can't be again –

a lesson
it takes a lifetime to learn.

Warm beneath your eiderdowns
you'll sleep through the night of Hallowe'en

in this house or the other,
with your father or mother

and a harvest moon –
only one –

over the park, over the patio.
Be at peace, and know

that a parent's love cannot be halved
but rather doubled, multiplied –

so unwavering are
the ties of the heart.

As October steals into November,
here are words for you to remember,

little boy blue, little girl lavender.

Dementia

Has seized our marriage by the throat.
Made us snap and snarl and spit.
Slap. Shout. Hit.

Heart pounds. Door bangs.
Pace outside, let it settle.
It's summer, it's beautiful.

I pout, sulk.
Shrug. Sigh. Frown.
Who is this woman I've become?

The girl you married with long black hair.
Your honey-brown eyes, your voice, so warm.
Your trust. Mine.

It was good for a long time.
Now your gaze is veiled,
you wear someone else's smile.

Your voice wobbles,
anxious, edgy.
You're fidgety, crotchety.

Where's my flashlight,
my shoe horn, my book?
Where did you put

my cell phone, my glasses?
And now I've lost my *carte vitale*,
my *carte d'identité*!

Yes, husband, your identity
has been misplaced,
mishandled, misshapen,

slowly crumbling
like your old ski boots
we found years later

that fell apart in our hands
in an avalanche
of powder.

Fish

Caught in the present
like fish in a net.
Were we ever free?

Sometimes I wish
I could start over,
be light-hearted,

laugh with joy.
What else are lips for,
mouths, hearts, souls?

Now we gasp for air,
we thrash and squirm,
there's not room

enough for us both.
What binds us
is the struggle,

fish caught in a net
we didn't make
that is unmaking us.

K.

What comes next?
And after that? And then?
No set path, no

familiar cobblestones
or open doorways,
none. Doors

locked, windows shuttered.
Weren't they always?
The little house

with the blue shutters
I dreamed myself into –
an illusion. I see myself

in a tiny kitchen as through
the wrong end
of a pair of binoculars.

Where shall we go?
And how shall we get there?
Our future, yours and mine,

disappears around the bend.
Like K.
in the snowbound village,

striving to reach the castle.
Land surveyor who could not
gauge the land, shuttled

from one inn to another,
at last he descended
to the rooms of the barmaids

in the depths of yet another labyrinth,
suspended at the end
of an unfinished chapter.

The House Shrew

It crept inside unseen,
edged along the bay windows
on its toothpick paws,
hunched itself into a corner of the room.

A shrew is territorial, it seems.
It can't stand for a fellow shrew
to encroach on its space.
When threatened, it shrieks.

Our shrew emerged,
a tiny mammal in a foul mood.
Itching for a fight, it squeaked.
It twitched its nose

into a tweak,
bared its little row of teeth.
It wouldn't be coaxed
or appeased.

It cast blame. It called names.
The door was open
but it wouldn't leave.
There was no reason for it to flee

because the shrew was me.

Slippers

I rue the day
I bought you those

black leather mules
you clump around the house in

and won't abandon
at any price

though they slow you down
to an old man's

shuffle
you seem almost thankful

to adopt.
I guess

each slipper is a place
your foot

feels at home in –
unlike shoes

that are hard to put on
and shoelaces

you can no longer tie,
when at my request

you trail along behind me,
you who walked so fast,

on errands that take us
into this shop or that

when you'd rather be back
in the comfort

of your armchair.
That must be why

you tote your mules
on every outing

even if they stay
in the car,

while your life
gets smaller

and more confined
as it fits around

an ever-diminishing
version of you,

your world in a shoe,
your home in a slipper,

your bed snug
as a hand-knit sock.

Daylight Saving

Last day of February.
The sun is warmer, the light lasts longer.
In March they'll put the clocks ahead
and give us an extra daytime hour.
What will daylight save for us,
or save us for?

Evenings with Mika

We sit by the fire,
husband and wife. Night
fallen, tasks done
or left for tomorrow.
We don't speak.

You sit across from me,
stiff as a post
in your wicker armchair,
eyes wide open,
seeming not to blink.

What do you see ?
Your wife in a red wool dress
and on her lap, Mika,
our young tiger-striped cat
who thinks

that a half-hour
of purring
and kneading the crook
of my arm will yield
a cupful of milk...

Bird-watcher,
toy owl-pouncer,
finger-biter,
comfort-giver,
she fills the lack

in our house
that's no longer quite
a home. She's
my feline other
who's quick

to sense my moods,
as I do hers.
Is she truly a cat?
Yes, and a little bit more,
but that's a quirk

only cat lovers will admit.
You think I exaggerate.
I'm sure you're right.
You doze in your armchair.
I stroke our cat.

Le Quatrième Internationale

It was all the fault of your father, so you chose
Trotsky instead, whose treatises, in May '68,

had lost none of their relevance, you said, when you were
a student in Dijon, holding forth at meetings

with well-worn arguments and reasons. You were in
for the long haul, but the Stalinists, you claimed,

brought the strike to an end. Your whole life long
you've been a faithful son

to the workers' revolution, the long awaited dawn.
It's an indisputable position, your being in the right

when nothing has proved you wrong.
But history goes marching on

and all the lessons have been unlearned –
on that, we agree. And who am I to say

you've been misguided? It's just that the path
keeps circling back to the beginning.

Neither Marx nor Lenin nor Trotsky
could counter the weight of your father's tyranny.

And tyranny breeds irony.
What you fled from

caught up with you in the end,
like a messenger racing to overtake you,

coattails flying…
As a child you stood to attention.

Then you became your own authority,
and the authority became you.

So much for libre arbitre,
for the Lumières.

The lesson's come too late for you.
Enlightenment, such as it is,

will be your legacy
for us to sort through.

Everlasting

Time present and time past
Are both perhaps present in time future
And time future contained in time past.
                    T.S. ELIOT, *The Four Quartets*

Day never-ending.
You sit. You walk around the house.
You wait.
What do you wait for?

You don't know.
I don't know either. You sit.
I scurry. Phone calls. E-mails.
Appointments. Meals.

Time lies heavy on your hands,
ticks off the hours,
glues you to your chair.
It's almost more than I can bear.

I can't claim to know
what time is, I only know
I want the full portion –
like a pitcher of cream

brimming, overflowing,
all the precious drops...
Time counted and uncountable,
time everlasting,

lasting as long as our lives do.

Spice Cupboard

Juniper and clove,
thyme and tarragon.
Who can I depend upon?

Star anise and linden flower,
I went away, and even further.
I broke the hearts of my father and mother.

Rosemary and marjoram.
I married, we had a son
who stayed in the womb,

who wasn't born.
Sorrow of lemon balm.
Solace of hypericum.

Lavender and coriander.
We had a daughter
and another daughter.

Raspberry leaf, chamomile and cinnamon.
My first daughter has a daughter
and a son.

Cardamom and ginger root,
cumin and turmeric.
This is my second daughter's music.

Poppy seed and elderflower.
I'm not yet old,
but getting older.

Gingko, saffron and dill
will not cure
my husband's ills.

Marigold and rue,
hyssop and shepherd's wort.
All I haven't learnt.

Bay leaf, sage and caraway.
Which confers wisdom?
Which longevity?

Nasturtium and rose,
starflower and clover.
Flowers to think things over.

The Manor House

I know.
I've put you in purgatory

where there's nothing for you to do
but wait for the time to pass

in a white room
down a white hallway

with a white plastic bracelet
around your wrist.

Then one day your case comes up
and a place is found,

a pleasant one
for good behavior

during the first seven
decades of your life –

a three-storey mansion
with a fireplace and two cats,

a wide staircase and a park,
almost like home.

I'll never say
you'll be happy there.

But high up in the clouds,
it's you who'll be the weather

of our days, floating just above me,
wrapping me in mist,

showering me with sunlight,
with rainfall.

What else will you be?
A stair-climber, a night-pacer,

a day-dreamer.
Above all

a secret-keeper,
a guardian of silences

that string one past to another
in the watery colors

of an after-storm's glittering light.
And I know

that on a clear autumn day
with a steady breeze

the manor house will rise
like a hot-air balloon

loosed from its moorings,
and I'll wave and wave

to the faces peering from the windows,
searching for yours, your downcast

sorrowful eyes, my once-husband,
soul-mate whose soul was lost,

Amen.

Note

'Here' was written as a homage to the Danish
poet Inger Christensen (1935–2009) whose poem
'Alphabet', as translated by Susanna Nied, has been
an inspiration to me for many years.